The
Heart of a
Worshiper

McDougal & Associates

Servants of Christ and Stewards of the
Mysteries of God

God's Greatest
Love,

Best

The
Heart of a
Worshiper

Inspirational Writings

by

Chelsea L. Johnson

All Bible references are from the *Holy Bible,
King James Version,* public domain.

Original cover design by Bryan Parker,
No Greater Love Graphics, Atlanta, Georgia
1bryanparker@gmail.com

Published by:

McDougal & Associates
18896 Greenwell Springs Road
Greenwell Springs, Louisiana 70739
www.ThePublishedWord.com

McDougal & Associates is an organization dedicated to the
spreading of the Gospel of Jesus Christ to as many people as
possible in the shortest time possible.

ISBN 978-1-940461-41-0

Printed on demand in the US, the UK, and Australia
For Worldwide Distribution

Dedication

To God, my Father: You have been the Lover of my Soul in times when I couldn't speak a word with my mouth. While on the path to destiny, Lord, You inspired and birthed in me the creativity to write comforting and inspirational poetry. Thank You, Lord, for You are my God, who is always concerned about what concerns me.

To my wonderful and loving husband: You encouraged me over the years to be who God has called me to be. Even when I was struggling to find myself and purpose, you were there to say, "God has a plan for your life, and you will fulfill purpose." Thank you for loving me and being there for me every step of the way.

To my beautiful children, Darrell, Jr. and Cierra: Thank you for your encouragement. When it didn't look like this book would ever get published, you both would say, "Mom, you can do it, don't give up!" I appreciate you and love you both.

Acknowledgments

Special thanks is due to every minister, family member, friend and church member who took time to listen as I shared my thoughts and encouraged me to reach high, dig deep and birth the vision that is now at hand.

Contents

And thou shalt love the Lord thy God with all thy heart, and with all thy soul, and with all thy mind, and with all thy strength: this is the first commandment.   Mark 12:30

To know Him is to love Him,
And to love Him
Is to love yourself
... For you are made in the likeness
And the image of GOD.

Introduction

These inspirational writings were written over a period of three years, a time in my life when I longed for true intimacy with the Father, and it seemed as if life challenges were getting the best of me. As I began to put pen to paper, the challenges and trials before me and the struggles inside of me now took on a different perspective, and I begin to see things through a pair of new lenses God created just for me.

The words released brought a sense of encouragement, strength, hope and peace. They provided an avenue for me to escape from the reality that was before me. All the while, I was on a wonderful journey of discovering the beauty of God's love for me.

There were times when I would go sit by the water (a favorite place for me) and listen to the waves as they flowed. So much peace and serenity! "God, please don't leave me; stay close," were the words I would utter each day, and God would always reassure me, "Daughter, I will never leave you nor forsake you; I am here always."

Allow the words written in this book to give you the encouragement to keep it moving at all times, the strength to stand through adversity and pain and the adjustments life brings. Let them produce a love in you that will never fail, build trust to know that God is always there and flood your soul with the joy of being a child of the King.

The best is yet to come, and the glory of the Lord shall be unveiled in and through your life … and mine.

God said it, and so shall it be!

Chelsea Johnson
Baton Rouge, Louisiana

Serenity of Heart and Mind

Listen to the melody.
Listen to the song.
Sing out of a pure heart.
Sing to glorify the LORD.

Listen to the words.
Let your mind soar,
As the Holy Spirit takes control forevermore.

Such peace!
Songs of triumph and victory,
Worship the King,
Your Creator, your Maker, your everything.

Listen to the melody.
Let it take control.
Let it flow in and through you,
Forever ringing in your soul.

Feelings of Despair

Feelings of despair,
Uncertain about what is next
In and for your life,
Knowing that the promises of
God are "yes" and "amen,"
Holding on to the dream,
As Joseph did,
Never letting go,
To what he believed.

As Jacob wrestled with the angel,
And would not let go until God blessed him,
He was persistent to hold on,
Trying to understand
And figure things out
In this place called a *mind.*

What direction should you go?
What move should you make?
When your strength is gone
And your peace has run on
And left you in despair.

What shall you do?
What move should you make?
Or should you turn and just walk away,
Holding on to your most holy faith,
Treading and dog paddling
The waters that try to flood
The path to holiness?

Pressing forward,
Pressing for the high call,
Which is Christ Jesus.
Removing mountains,
Breaking and tearing down walls,
You will make it through.
For God will see you through it all.

Despair must go.
We are not defeated.
Surely Satan knows.
Conqueror is our name,
And the LION OF JUDAH in us continues to reign.

The battles is not ours;
But it is the LORD's.
Cast everything upon the altar,
For He shall take care of it all.

Removing every frown,
Allowing the Holy Spirit to bring a smile.
He rocks us in His arms,
Hearing His voice say,
"Just be strong and hold on,
For I will never leave you alone."
Let us now release and let go
Those dreadful FEELINGS OF DESPAIR.

A Reality

A vision that one day
People will come together,
Both the young and the old,
Working together, hand in hand.
Unity is key, for this to become
The world's reality.

Building each other's hopes and dreams,
Spreading life and not death,
Fulfilling purpose and destiny each,
Individually and corporately.
People of all color and nationality,
Traveling together from one part of
The world to another,
Demonstrating what is written
In the volumes of the Book called the Bible.

Children of every nation,
Playing, singing, laughing together,
All in one accord,
Expressing the gift that is above all gifts,
The ultimate gift called Love.

Love sees no color,
It has no creed.
Jesus died for you and me,
Unconditional and free.
That was His love displayed for eternity.

Yes, this is the dream,
But soon ... it will no longer be a dream,
Just simply a REALITY.

Straightjacket

The STRAIGHTJACKET, color of white,
And, oh, so extremely tight,
It grips your arms,
Tightens them across your chest,
To keep you in a place of restriction.

A straightjacket is not a good feel.
So tied and tangled up, unable to move,
You do not understand why this has to be.

Trying to please everyone,
Everyone except the One who really matters,
Feeling hindered to express your true feelings,
Saying to yourself, "Who am I trying to be?"
Oh, then you realize ...
"I'm trying to be everybody but me!"
The struggle is real.
Your insides want to cry
To release the pain you feel inside.

People would say,
"How could you feel this way?
You're blessed!

Your family is blessed!"
And you would surely agree.
But you're still human
And trying so hard to just be,
A mighty woman of GOD
Filled with purpose,
Striving and moving toward
Fulfilling a great destiny.

Guessing sometimes, "Yes, LORD,
I'm being selfish about the way I feel."
It would appear you are
Always talking just about you.
So, with that in mind,
You choose to stay quiet
And stay locked in this STRAIGHTJACKET.

If you try to get out,
You feel put-down or belittled.
The still, small voice of the LORD says,
"You have the power to pull the wall down."
But you really just don't know how.

The STRAIGHTJACKET seems
To get tighter and tighter.
At times it loosens just enough
To let you know you are still here,
But yet not totally set free.

Frustrated and confused, you ask God,
"Who do You want me to be?"
He replies lovingly,
"Only who I created you to be."

You answer, "ME, Lord?"
It appears ME offends others
And is not complete.
Confusion has now become your name,
Trying to be one way,
But being perceived as another.

You know God hears you
And this Straightjacket you feel
Is only temporary.
This will not always be.
This is not His plan for you.

You will break free from this Straightjacket
And find your true identity.
Victory lies deep within you.
You were created by the King in His image.
Soon all will see the discovery
That has been made,
A wonderful, loving woman,
Created in the image of God,
And that discovery is The Real Me!

The Great Spiritual Ball

The royal invitation has been sent.
You have been chosen,
And you have been called,
Summoned by the King.

Put away your rags, those fleshly things,
And clothe yourself in His righteousness.
Be washed in the blood.
For on this fateful day,
We are all gathered in one accord.

Come one! Come all!
Those who accept the LORD,
Salvation is the key
To come in and behold the rejoicing.

The table has been set,
Right before all of your enemies.
Eat from the table
God has set for you.

The music plays
A melody of sweet peace and serenity.

We are clothed in garments of praise,
Singing, dancing,
Letting the joy of the LORD reign.

Then, at the drop of a hat, the music stops.
The trumpets line up in a row
With the heavenly angels and began to blow.

As we stand in awe,
Awaiting the arrival of the King,
Upon His great white horse,
He enters in with His face all aglow.

Such grace!
Such royalty!
Come one! Come all!
To a gathering of the saints,
To meet the one and only King.
Come one! Come all!
To THE GREAT SPIRITUAL BALL.

Majesty

Precious LORD,
How excellent is Thy name,
My Father and my Friend.
Speak one word
And I'll watch the wondrous works begin.

The Giver of Life, the Restorer of my Soul,
My heart leaps with joy.
The Holy One sits high upon His throne.
Royalty is what He displays.

His name is Jesus, our King!
Alone that name says everything.
Such grace! Such mercy!
How can one turn and walk away?

He rules and reigns upon the throne
And sits by the right hand of the Father,
With a scepter in His hand.
Angels singing, "Holy! Holy!
Worthy is the Lamb!
Jesus Christ, the King!"

What a beautiful sight!
So marvelous to behold!
The Lamb of God,
The Chief Cornerstone.

The colors of purple, blue,
Orange, red, green and gold
Surround His Kingdom,
All with such a glorious glow.

The music plays melodies of worship
Unto the Lamb that was slain.
The blood He shed for us
To live life more abundantly.

The angels bow down
With trumpets in their hands.
Hark, the herald angels sing,
Releasing a loud sound
Indescribable to the carnal man,
As we prepare the entrance
Of the Prince of Peace,
The Lord of Lords,
Our Father, Emmanuel.

Open your spiritual eyes,
For the flesh will not be able to see
The wonderful place
GOD Himself has prepared for you and me.

Crucify the flesh
And take this spiritual journey,
For worship is the key.

The veil has been ripped,
The price has been paid.
You're free to come enter in.
Come into the Holy of Holies
With the King.

A Spiritual Life-Giver

It begins with intimacy
Between a man and a woman.
A seed is planted inside a woman,
And the process to bring forth life begins.

There is also an intimacy
That is produced in the Spirit,
Between GOD and me.
He has planted His seed,
Which is His living Word,
Uncompromised and complete.
A SPIRITUAL LIFE-GIVER
Is what we were all created
To be originally.

The incubation stage is over.
Growth has already begun.
The time of release is fast approaching.
The baby is kicking,
Ready to be introduced into society.

Just as a mother delivers a baby,
So we must deliver His Word

And fulfill His purpose in this world,
Pushing through the hurt and the pain.
When the process is over,
Watch the joy it brings!

Even in the natural, when a baby is born,
Everyone comes to see this new life
That was brought forth through thee.
In the beginning,
The baby has some traits of you,
But in the end, this baby will only have
Traits of Me.

Be not afraid, nor abort the seed,
This gift you have been given
By God Almighty.
Protect and keep it
From every attack of the enemy.
For in this seed lies your purpose and destiny.
For in you is My seed.

Remember, people will come and see
The baby that looks like you,
But the character and attributes
Are completely of Me.
A Spiritual Life-Giver we all
Have been chosen to be.

Thunder and Lightning

A beautiful day,
The sun is shining bright.
Birds are flying and singing songs of praise.
Trees are swaying from side to side,
Dancing to the breeze that God provides.

Children are out playing.
All is calm, but out afar,
Here comes the storm.

The clouds roll in.
The sky is covered by darkness.
The birds can no longer be found.
Lightning strikes aloud.
Thunder roars,
And the rain now begins to pour,
Lasting for several minutes,
An hour or even more.

Time continues to pass on.
Finally, the sun finds its place,
And our normal way of life
Starts all over again.

Even in the Spirit realm,
This is how we are.
When everything is going fine,
We are happy, joyful and full of life,
Praising, singing, rejoicing
Because He is LORD!

Then, as the storm of life
Begins to approach,
Our minds become darkened
By the clouds.
Now we are all in disarray.

Chaos sets in,
As we search for some shelter or relief.
The thunder roars, the lightning strikes,
And the door to fear has
Swung open wide in your life.
We look for shelter,
For someone to help,
Exhausted from trying to work things out
In our own strength.

God is standing on the shore of our heart,
Saying, "Oh, ye of little faith,
Stand still and be sure in Whom you serve.

I am with you
Through the storm and the rain,
Through all the discomfort and the pain.
Let not your heart be troubled,
Neither be perplexed,
For the storms in your life
Have been approved by Me.
I'm getting your attention,
Can't you see?"

"The thunder, the lightning came to distract.
Stay focused and receive the promise.
Throw out fear and keep your eyes on Me.
The storms must come
To produce a new anointing.
Glory to glory is where you must go.
Don't stop! I am in control!"

There is always shelter from the storm,
Not in your family, nor in a friend,
But the shelter is found
Through worship
And placing your trust in HIM.
Storms come in the natural
To replenish the earth,

To wash away the old and bring forth
What is needed for new things to grow.

So, in the Spirit, the same principle applies.
Storms come in the Spirit
To keep God's promise alive,
Washing away everything unlike Him,
Making perfect, establishing, strengthening
And settling a great new you.

Be patient!
Just wait and see.
The storm won't last always.
And behind the storm awaits
A bright and glorious day.

Expressions of Love

Jesus, I love You
With all of my heart.
No matter what,
I will serve You.

Jesus, I love You,
Not because You first loved me,
But because it was meant to be.

Jesus, I love You.
My heart cries, "Holy! Holy!" unto Thee.
I long just to worship at Your feet,
In total surrender and reverence to the King.

Jesus, I love You
More and more each day.
Your grace and mercy toward me
Has been so ever faithful.
You provide everything I need,
Working things out
Beyond my comprehension and belief.

I am thankful You are always there for me.
Jesus, I love You.

Not Denied

A heart filled with disappointments,
Standing in faith on what you believe,
Running after a never-ending dream,
Only to be disappointed again.
But everything is not what it seems.

How do you hold on?
How do you keep the faith?
Questions fill your mind,
As joy ceases to abide.

The pain feels so strong and real,
Until you cannot even utter
A word of comfort or relief.
God is your refuge!
He is your strength!

But you say, "What is the next step?
What move should you make?
I'm attempting, pressing
And pushing to succeed,
Only to be met with disappointment again."

You look in the mirror
With tears in your eyes,
To determine, "Is it me?
Am I the hindrance I see?"
Suddenly scales begin to fall.
God allows you to see beyond the walls.

To your amazement, reality hits.
That disappointment you feel
Is not sent from GOD,
But sent from the enemy,
To fill your mentality with wrong thinking.

Dry your eyes! Wipe your face,
And stand in faith!
No more disappointment.
Only the great pursuit
To your GOD-given happiness.

Watch GOD move!
For He is not a GOD of disappointment.
But He will fulfill His purpose
And bring forth your glorious
And prosperous destiny.

A Place Called Rest

How can you enter into the rest of the LORD
When all seems to be going wrong?
The seasons are changing.
Nothing is remaining.
It seems things have truly dried up,
And you look around.
All you can see is the cloudiness
That is in front and in back of you.
The way seems so unclear,
But you hear GOD say, "Rest and be still!"

Your hearts skips a beat,
As you try to figure out
What is really happening.
What is on the horizon?
Why can't you see?
And you beg the LORD
To provide the answers you need.

Martha worked,
As she prepared for the visitation of the King.
Mary sat at Your feet
And listened to every word You released.
Now, Your pleasure was in Mary.

Martha was only getting
Everything You needed.
From this scenario, we learn
That intimacy is key.

It's time to rest.
We must sit at His feet and learn
That He is God Almighty.
Enter into that place of peace,
Even when storms seem
To be present all around.
Worry not, for at His feet
Is where you should be.
Then we can enter A Place Called Rest.

Transition

To move from one level to the next,
Moving from the familiar to the unfamiliar.
Are you ready to go?
Are you ready to soar?
No more comfort!

The doors have been closed,
And nothing will cause them to unfold,
Until you move to the place
That is unknown to you.
By My Spirit you will know
That there is a place where you must go.

Move without fear!
Move by faith!
For I am ready to take you to that place
Where the blessings overflow
And your labor is not in vain.

No more headaches!
No more pain!
A season that has truly been ordained.
Moving forward, never looking back.
To look back means to stumble and fall.

Pressing forward is the thing
You should strive for.
Leaning not to your own understanding,
But relying on Me for this transitioning.

Trust Me and see
The place that I will take thee,
Not by power,
Not by might,
But by the Spirit of the LORD.
And then you will say,
"I am moving.
It's GOD, the family and me."

Those who may say
That it is not Me orchestrating everything ... ,
Just remember the talk that You and I had,
And know it is only Me
Taking thee to this new place called There.

Lost in the Field

On a bright, sunny day,
The phone rings,
And the person on the other end says,
"We cannot find your child.
He is nowhere to be found."
Your heart triples in beat,
And you drop to your knees.
Chaos is all around,
People trying to assist, to calm you down.

A still, small voice speaks to your friend.
It says, "The boy is covered by My blood.
No need to fear."
But fear grips her tongue,
She is unable to speak words
That will surely bring you
Some comfort and relief.
Your spirit and flesh begin to war,
Fighting for a place in your head.
Unsure of what to do
All you can say is, "Jesus, help me!"

The phone rings again,
And the voice on the other end
Begins to sigh and say,
"It was a mistaken identity.
Your child has been found.
Both children had the same name,
And both are accounted for."

Such unwanted drama,
Unexpected, you see!
But think about how many of GOD's children
Are lost in the field,
Lost, with no identity,
Hopelessly roaming around.
What a blessing that,
In the natural, both children were found!

Now GOD is steadily calling
For those that are still lost in the field.
We must listen to His voice, do His will,
That they, too, will be safe,
Living under the shadow of His wings
And no longer LOST IN THE FIELD.

Worry

In the season when nothing seems
To be going right,
Finances are attacked,
And you're doing your best
Trying not to look back,
Thinking you are doing everything wrong,
Worrying because there is so much to be done.
Trouble seems to be on every side.
Emotions are on a roller-coaster ride.
What is the lesson to be learned?
GOD is on your side

When all seems to be going wrong.
Knowing His promises are "yes" and "amen,"
The only thing for you to do is stand,
Casting every care upon Him,
Leaning not to your own understanding.
Worry will take away all of your joy.
Worry will make you wish
You had never been born.
Worry is a sin unto the LORD.
So, why not put your trust in the name
That is above every name?

Believe in change!
Learn to be worry free,
Free from fear of what will be.
Trust in the LORD,
For He is truly with thee.
And if He is with thee,
Tell me, then who can be against thee?!

The Storm Is Over

THE STORM IS OVER
And you say, "LORD, thank You,
I survived the constant rain
That came my way.
But can I survive the water
That has been left behind?
THE STORM IS OVER,
But when will the water recede?"

THE STORM IS OVER, but you say,
"God, I can't see the land
Flowing with milk and honey
That You have promised me.
THE STORM IS OVER,
But when will the dove send me
A piece of hope or a piece of a dream?
When will the dove bring
hope from the fig tree?
LORD, as far as my natural eye can see,
So much water surrounds me.
You look all around,
And, God, You cannot be found."

Expecting every day
For change to take place,
But when you wake up every morning
And even as you go through the day,
You say, "I know GOD is going to make a way."
As you look out the window of your heart,
You see that all of that water
Is still surrounding you.
Much to your disappointment,
Things are still the same.
There has been no change.
You begin to encourage yourself,
And your spirit begins to rise.
You are trying to keep the dream alive.

THE STORM IS OVER,
And now you say,
"LORD, when will the water recede?"
One day you know your miracle will arrive.
Standing in faith,
Keeping watch at the gate of your heart,
Knowing that the dove sent out in faith
Will return with a token
Of hope and not dismay.

"God, You are faithful,
And Your Word is true.
I trust and believe
That every promise will come true."
Why?
Because you now believe,
THE STORM IS OVER!

The Heart of a Worshiper

As I arise to the dawn of a new day,
My eyes behold the wonder of His love,
For He is the Creator of everything.
Undeniable praise begins to flow from my lips,
As my mind takes a paradigm shift,
To seek the heart and mind of the King.

As the winds of the Holy Spirit blow,
My eyes begin to close.
As I take a deep breath
And allow my spirit to soar,
Tears of joy and peace begin to flow.

My knees begin to shake and buckle,
As I fall to the ground
With my face in my hands.
Due to the weight of His glory,
I can no longer stand.
As I allow this flesh of mine
To be crucified and die,
I lift my head
With my arms stretched wide open
Up toward the sky.

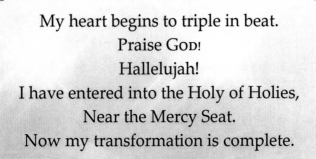

My heart begins to triple in beat.
Praise GOD!
Hallelujah!
I have entered into the Holy of Holies,
Near the Mercy Seat.
Now my transformation is complete.

No longer a stony heart,
But now a heart of flesh,
THE HEART OF A WORSHIPER lives
On the inside of me.

Holding On

Days have gone by,
Years have come and gone,
And yet you are still holding on,
Holding on to every promise made,
Holding on to every word God said.

Many have come and gone.
New relationships have now been formed.
Oh, Lord, I am still holding on,
Wondering every day,
"What can you do
To repay our God who is so good?"

All I can do is to continue
To stay focused on this road called Life,
Knowing that we are never alone.
It's for that reason that you and I
Are still Holding On.

The Eagle

Joy and peace ... ,
These are the things GOD has given unto thee.
No matter what you see
With your natural eyes,
Your spirit will continue to soar,
As the eagle flies,
Through the clouds in the sky,
Flying with no care and no despair,
With his wings spread afar.
Strong and mighty, that's who you are.

Joy and peace ... ,
Even when the storms of life try to overtake,
We shall be like that eagle,
Flying over difficult situations,
Flying over obstacles,
Flying into complete victory.

Powerful and strong,
Bold and courageous,
That's the Eagle, the Holy Spirit
Who abides in each of us.

Patience

God, are You there today?
Please be our Captain on the raging sea.
We sit and wait on an answer from You,
Patiently, believing in the Word
That is ever so true.
"Trust and be still," is what You say.

We wait and wait,
But nothing seems to be happening.
Emotions are in an uproar.
The mind never ceases.
But, GOD, our Father, we still trust Thee.

Inside, tears flow.
The soul releasing the frustrations
Of today and days gone astray.
"Be strong," you tell yourself.
Knowing that things are working
Together for the good,
Still not understanding
What is going on.

To sit and wait,
Is it right? Or is it wrong?
You said, "Faith without works is dead."
Searching to find the answers,
But to no success,
Hearing You say, "In your own strength
Is not the way."
So, leaning, depending
And casting every care upon You,
LORD, we need Your favor.

Peace and stability ... ,
Striving to keep our minds stayed on Thee
In order to have total victory.
PATIENCE, we call your name.
PATIENCE, please help me to sustain.

Within

How can I express what I truly feel inside,
A love for my husband,
A love for my children,
A love for my GOD above?
My heart filled with desire
To express the love that is so inspiring:
To give a hug and not push away,
To give a smile instead of a frown.

What in my life makes the void seem so real,
That keeps me so tied down,
And makes me so unable to give?
My soul cries out at some points of the day.
I feel something missing,
"Oh, Father, help me!" I pray.

I look at the lake
And how beautiful it is,
The peace and serenity ...
That's what I need within.
I ask myself, "Is it something I did
That makes me feel so unfulfilled?"
But God says, "No."
He has forgiven every sin.

Again, I stand before the water
Day after day,
Questioning the void that stands in my way.
I've reached out to so many,
And God has said, "No,
The one that I will send
Will have fire and yet a stability.
Don't you know?"

That virtuous woman is who I want to be.
"So, God, I ask,
Bring her forth in me."
"Lord," I pray,
Remove every restraint.
Tear down the walls.
God, the emptiness goes so deep,
But I am a conqueror.
From this day forth,
With Your help alone,
I'll trust you, Lord.
And, hopefully, they will see
How much I love them
And my God Almighty!"

The Character of GOD

Oh, how beautiful the flower appears to be!
After the process of the four seasons,
Is there still a beauty we will see?
But, like the flower,
During the four seasons of life,
A change is taking place in me.
Winter, spring, summer and fall,
God is constantly working during them all.

Through the cold,
When you feel GOD is not near,
Just around the corner
Are the spring showers of blessings.
And you have no fear.

Now summer is here,
And the furnace of life
Has been turned up a little hotter.

During the fall,
Everything that is unfruitful must die,
To make room
For what must be produced and stay alive.

Through it all,
I must stay connected to the True Vine.
No more desolate land!
I must be fruitful and multiply.

A year has passed,
And the process begins again.
But how thankful I am to know
There is still a beauty we see,
Because the character of GOD
Has been produced in me.

The fruits of the Spirit:
Love, peace, joy, longsuffering,
Temperance, gentleness,
Goodness, faith and meekness ...
That is what we all must have
To show forth THE CHARACTER OF GOD.

Run to the Water

RUN TO THE WATER,
Where nothing bothers you,
And the Spirit of GOD
Waits to talk with you.

RUN TO THE WATER,
Beautiful and blue.
There the Holy Spirit waits for you.

RUN TO THE WATER,
Where the Spirit of GOD abides.
Allow Him to take you
On a spiritual journey,
Forever changing your heart and mind.

Captivity

Your destiny and purpose
Awaits your release.
Satan can only hold you captive
If you chose to be.
God has already released you.
He has already set you free.

So, why choose to have chains holding thee?
God is a Deliverer.
He's already proved
He is a Redeemer.
GOD will re-establish you.

Bondage to the thoughts
Of things that use to be,
The old you and the old ways,
Let GOD redirect you.
Putting away those things
That are behind you
And pressing for those things
That are in front of you.

Wake up and see,
The enemy wants to capture thee.
Wake up and see,
God has already freed thee.

Sins of the past are far behind you.
Sin has the power to separate and bind;
God has the power to redeem.
Repentance is required
For this to be achieved.
Then, shackles are broken;
Chains are released.
Washed by the blood,
Free from Captivity.
Thank God, He loves you
And has set you free.

Dreams

Now I lay me down to sleep.
I pray to the LORD to rest in peace.
But thoughts never cease
Of things that use to be.
And the enemy tries to recapture me.
Imaginings, illusions of things gone by,
Feelings of shame,
Distrust and every other unclean thing
Steadily run behind me and try to hold me.

Fighting to keep my true identity,
Reminding myself that the old man
Can and will no longer be.
Sometimes, GOD, the fight overwhelms me.
No longer captive,
I've been totally set free.
This is what my GOD tells me!

I rejoice in the newness that is set before me,
But why must we deal with the images
That haunt our peace,
Tossing and turning as we sleep?
Watch out,
Satan is out to destroy and hinder
The destiny that lies in you and me.

But, thank GOD,
We already have the victory.
But how do you fight
The dreams that come in the night?
The past is gone, and never to return.
Now, let's finally move on.
Binding and loosing ... this is the key,
Leaving all of those things far behind me.

You have repented to the LORD,
And He forgave thee.
Now, no more condemnation,
For His grace and mercy
Have been extended toward you,
Can't you see?

Close the door to the thoughts of the past.
Turn the key and lock away every hurt,
Disappointment and iniquity.
Now, walk into the purpose and destiny
That GOD Himself has waiting
And prepared for thee.

The Blessings of the LORD

How sweet it is to know that I am blessed,
Above measure,
Above hope,
As far as my mind can conceive,
As far as my natural eye can see,
Speaking those things into existence.
God is still blessing me.

I serve a GOD of increase.
He will enlarge my territory
And keep me from every iniquity.

He is faithful!
He is true!
There is nothing He will keep from you!
Believe and receive
All that He has in store for thee.

Do not worry!
Do not fret!
Even though the winds may blow,
Be strong and unmovable.

Wait upon the LORD,
The Renewer of your strength.
Move only as He commands,
To walk into the new season at hand.

For everyone will see
That God has truly blessed thee.
The hand of the LORD,
The blessings of GOD
Are forever upon thee and even me.

When I Dance

WHEN I DANCE, there is a joy within
That can never be touched.
WHEN I DANCE, there is a peace
That passes all understanding.
No pain, no struggles, flowing in the Spirit,
Like water flows down a stream,
Unstoppable, unreachable,
Another dimension, just GOD and me.

WHEN I DANCE, problems, worries,
And unbearable weights
Are no longer an issue.
While I dance, O, watch and see,
The flair of the garment,
The colors that represents the King.
Lost in the music created just for Him,
A twirl, a kick, a leap, a spin ...
All created by Him.

Come, go with me, to the dancer's place
Of true serenity.
Close your eyes and see a dancer,
Flowing in the wind
With a melody in her heart
And ministry throughout her body.

Such grace!
Such peace!
Dancing ... ,
It's God and me.

The Father's Love

THE FATHER'S LOVE,
Unconditional and true.
In good times and bad times,
He promised He will never leave you.

THE FATHER'S LOVE
Goes beyond measure.
Despite what we say or do,
He will never forsake you.

THE FATHER'S LOVE,
Purity not emotionally,
Always in the midst of thee,
Our GOD, the Father, Creator of everything.

THE FATHER'S LOVE
Heals the hurt, removes the pain,
Repairs the breach and restores the heart.
Grace He extends beyond all knowing.
Mercy He gives when tears are flowing.

THE FATHER'S LOVE,
So genuine and so true.
It will be forever
Wrapped around you.

Centerpiece

The potter and the clay ...
On the wheel of life, the clay is laid.
He sits on His throne,
He's shaping, molding and pulling away
Every unnecessary piece of the clay,
Transforming it in such a beautiful way.
It begins to make an image
That brings a smile to His face.

That image is now a reflection of Him.
Jesus is the Potter, and we are the clay.
Through our trials of life,
He makes us into His image of righteousness.
Once the stages are complete,
He then displays His beautiful creation
And calls it His CENTERPIECE.

On the table of life, we are then placed
To encourage the others
Who must come this way.
This is the process
That GOD has prepared for you and for me.

In your due season,
You shall sit so gloriously,
High up on the table of life,
As God's CENTERPIECE.

Make sure your foundation is firm.
One little hit
And the CENTERPIECE may slip and fall.
But the Potter,
So compassionate and patient is He,
Gently picks up you and me.
Now restoration must proceed.
Repairs are made.
Bruises are removed.
Back in one piece.
Totally restored.

A new foundation has been laid.
The table has been reset,
And your place has been saved.
Ordained before the foundation of the world,
He has already commanded you and me
To be the gift,
Our heavenly Father's CENTERPIECE.

Forever Yours

A willing vessel,
I am here.
Do as You please.
Even if I do not understand
What You tell me,
And I don't even agree,
It is good to know
That You know what is best for me.
Even when I cannot see what lies before me,
You will not lead me astray.
But You will direct my path in every way.

I am FOREVER YOURS.
You are always with me,
Even when I cannot feel You near.
My heart always remains secure,
That You will never leave nor forsake me.

I am FOREVER YOURS,
Through the good and the bad,
Through the pain and hurt,
But I never let go.
You've bought me with a price
That can never be compared.

Nothing I could do
Could ever repay You.
Every day of my life
I am Forever Yours.

The Love of God

THE LOVE OF GOD
Is so unconditional and undying.
GOD is the GOD of Heaven and Earth.
He created me in His image
And for His glory to be displayed in the earth.

He has created me a worthy vessel.
GOD has made me His centerpiece,
Shaped, molded and made
To give Him glory and honor,
To praise Him
With every fiber of my being.

GOD is love.
Through the suffering and the trials,
Through the uncertainties,
Challenges and pain,
GOD is still love.
He loves me even when I don't love myself.

His love is never based
On unrealistic conditions
And unreachable expectations.
His love never changes.

God extends His grace and mercy
Because He loves me.

If it had not been
For the grace and mercy of GOD,
Where would I be?
He loves me so much
That He gave His life a ransom
That I might have the right
To the tree of life.

THE LOVE OF GOD,
So great and mighty,
Without borders and boundaries,
Ever flowing, ever near,
No matter when I think He is not here
And not listening.

When I look to the right and find Him not,
When I look to the left,
In front and behind
And find Him not,
He promised He would always be there,
Even in my disobedience,
Even in not trusting and doubting,
In fear and insecurity,

Jehovah, the Redeemer
Jehovah, my faithful King,
Is still there.

THE LOVE OF GOD,
Who could explain it?
Who could understand it?
All I can do is be grateful and accept it.

2 + 1 = 3

The love between a man and a woman
Can be tested and tried by the trails of life.
Remember the day the bride
Stood at the back of the church,
Awaiting the sound of the organ,
To proceed down the aisle before her,
To meet the man
Whom GOD created to be her husband?

The minister stands in front of them,
To have them repeat the words
That should stand for all eternity.
What a magical moment!
Such joy! Such peace!
The ceremony ... , GOD created to be.

God is right in the midst of them,
Saying, "Here are My children
Being united as one in Me."

Then, when the ceremony is over,
Night begins to fall,
And everyone has gone home.
A new day arrives,
And now begins the new life
Between him and me.
Now we are truly husband and wife.

As days go on and years pass by,
The trials and challenges come to divide.
Children are born.
The reality of life begins to take form,
Distractions on every hand
Difficulties we just don't understand.

Staying strong in the faith,
Fighting to keep what is yours,
GOD's promises will not be unfulfilled.
There is more for us than against us,
As long as there is unity.

Pray day after day,
Never ceasing and speaking
What the Word says:
"What GOD has joined together,
Let no man put asunder!"
2 + 1 = 3.

The man and woman represent the two.
They, joined together in GOD's sight, are one,
And GOD covering them makes three.
Because of this, we will never be defeated
Because it's GOD first,
My husband second and thirdly me.

Don't Lose Ground

Though the trials still come,
There are previous battles you have won.
Don't lose the ground
You have purchased with your tears.
God has delivered you.
Are you going to give in?

The night you did not sleep,
You tossed and turned
And cried out,
"GOD, help me to be strong."
There is a price you will pay,
For the anointing to be displayed.
The process is set just for you,
Tailor-made by the King,
To create a new you.

DON'T LOSE GROUND.
Move forward,
Always pressing,
Always claiming what is to be,
Declaring and decreeing,
And not reliving what used to be.

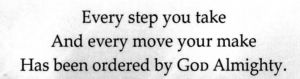

Every step you take
And every move your make
Has been ordered by God Almighty.

Don't Lose Ground,
For it has been purchased by your tears
And all the heartaches of yesteryears.
Again, Don't Lose Ground.

In My Weakness

Father God, In My Weakness
You are made strong.
When I just want to throw in the towel
And say, "It isn't so,"
You pick me up and say,
"Doubtfulness has to go."
And You bid me to come on a little more.

My thoughts are so confused.
No one in this world is above You.
I commit myself to You,
To be used in every way,
Even when I can't see my way,
When everything around seems so strange.
In My Weakness, You are made strong.

There is none like You in the heavens
And none like You in the earth.
Authority and majesty is what You represent.
I buckle in my knees,
Because the pressure is too strong for me.
I lay awake at night,
Trying to figure out,
"What can I do to make it right?"

But then I hear You say,
"What is too heavy for you
Cast upon Me,
For I care for you."

In My Weakness, You are made strong.
When all is said and done
And my agenda and my will
Is totally destroyed,
You say, "Thank you, daughter.
Now I can move in the midst of you,
Because in your weakness
I am made strong."

From My Heart to Yours

A man filled with love and compassion,
A man filled with hopes and dreams,
That he shall see fulfilled,
A man that has a heart truly after God,
Never letting go of the dreams
That have been placed inside ...
Strong and mighty, that's who you are!

Underneath your strength
Lies a man, so gentle and kind,
Ordained, while in your mother's womb,
To be mine.

Made with the craftiness of God,
Strategically put together in every way,
You are the man I love today and every day.

It brings joy to my life,
Just knowing you are near.
Being wrapped in your arms,
Feeling so secure.

How great the day God had you on His mind
And placed you in this earth
To be a part of mankind!

He created you as handsome as can be,
Unique, charming and full of creativity.
Filled with God's power and authority,
Musically inclined,
Full of melody and divine harmonies,
You were destined to be mine.
The father of my children,
A man of honor, grace and integrity,
My love for you is real,
So don't ever forget it!

We have cried together.
We have laughed together
And have disagreed in more ways than one.
You were equipped
And ordained to fulfill my every need.
I am truly honored
To have been chosen by God
To be your wife, your lover,
And your friend.
I am so thankful that you are
And forever will be my HUSBAND.

The Miracles

I wake up every morning
And see the miracle God has given.
For I beheld myself in the mirror.
To see He has given me life,
Breath and the activity of my limbs,
I can shout the victory
Over everything that tries to hinder me.
You want to see a miracle?
Just take a look at me.

Take a look at the transformation.
God has created newness with me.
Old things are passed away.
Behold, all things are new.
My mind has been transformed,
And my heart has been changed.
God has provided everything I need.
I am thankful and grateful
For the promotion
That has taken place within me.

Careful never to let
A boastful spirit be my friend,
Because anything not of GOD is my enemy.
Staying forever humble is the key to victory.
It's a miracle just to be me.
To walk in purpose and destiny,
Being bold and confident,
Knowing the true and living GOD
Is working throughout
And within me.

Even though there have been trials
And challenges in my life,
Some devastating and sometimes unbearable
And not a good sight to see,
You become so weak
And fall to your knees.
Satan believes that he has the victory.
Oh, but little does he know
That down on your knees
Is where you belong.
When you are weak, GOD is strong.
I am blessed all the day long.

So many miracles!
I just don't have the words
To express my gratitude
For a Father who displays grace and mercies
That renew every morning.
I run to the closet
Where my royal garments,
That represent the King,
Are neatly hung,
Reachable at any given moment,
And begin to dance to the melody
That is put before me.
Giving love to my Father,
With my heart ever on display,
Thanking Him for THE MIRACLES
Of yesterday and today
And those that are stored
In GOD's heavenly bank,
Awaiting the opportunity
To come my way.

The Goldfish

An open field is what I see.
And there is a big goldfish running after me.
I try to get away.
Fear is all over me.
The faster I run,
The more he comes.
I look back to see.
Oh, my God!
This big goldfish is still chasing me!
What do I do?
Who can I call?
Do I fight?
Or do I just stand still?
My face is filled with fear,
And no one is near,
Just me, the fish, and the open field.

Much to my delight, I awoke.
It was just a dream.
But, LORD, it felt so real.

I looked around the room.
And there was nothing to see,
Just my dear, sweet husband,
Soundly sleeping next to me.

I called someone who is very dear to me,
And began to tell her about the dream
Of a big goldfish chasing me.
She said, "The fish represents prosperity"
And that prosperity was chasing me,
Trying to catch up,
But I was running in fear
Of what would be.
She then encouraged me
To just stand still
And let the blessing of the LORD
Overtake me.

A New Heart

David said, *"God, create in me a clean heart,
and renew a right spirit within me."*

"God, give me a new heart."
That's my cry unto Thee.
Renew and transform my mind within me.
Remove everything that is unlike Thee.
Inside/out is the work that needs to be.
Overhaul my inner being,
To bring forth all the life-giving
Attributes that are needed.

No matter how good we look on the outside,
We dress up this fleshly body
With new clothes, a new style of hair,
And makeup galore,
But everything in us is not being observed.
God, you look on the heart
And not on the outward appearance of man.
For the ways of man seemeth right,
But GOD weigheth the spirits.

We are on a pursuit
Of an image that is not real and true
With our big hats, coach bags
And designer suits.
Thinking this is the image of GOD,
The image of prosperity,
We say, "I am a representative of GOD,
Can't you see?"
But you say, "Help them, for this is not Me!"

Perfection is what we seek
And the acceptance of man.
In our hearts we say,
"Look, world, this platform is just for me."

The children of Israel,
From what they thought,
Had an image of You.
From the wealth You provided for them,
They resurrected an image
Of a golden calf,
As a representation of the Almighty.
In other words,
Their mind was not renewed.
The traditions of man
Were still deep in their souls.

Miracles had been performed
Right before their very eyes,
But when all was said and done,
Their mind was not transformed,
And their heart was not brand new.

Moving out everything,
That is not a true image of You.
Repentance for our ignorance.
You say, "Study to show thyself approved."

Encouraged in my spirit,
Knowing You would not withhold
Any good thing from me,
Seeking Your face and not Your hand,
Knowing You for myself in a real way,
Compassion, mercy and grace
Is bestowed upon my every day.

As I go through the surgery of a new heart
Being created more and more each day,
I rejoice in knowing
The Physician has a steady hand.
Because my trust lies only in the Man
Whose name is above every name.
And His name is Jesus!

A Tug of War

Are your ready to fight?
Or ready to give in?
The battle begins in the mind.

On the battlefield,
Satan attempts to come in
Like a thief in the night.

When life is going fine
And all is going your way,
Your mind is a terrible thing to waste.
The mind, where Satan
And his demons seek
To conqueror and destroy,
Trying to take your mind
And your soul, all at the same time.

The flesh and the spirit are constantly at war.
Satan does not follow the rules.
He is a cheater, a liar, and he will lose.

Overwhelmed is now how you feel,
Tired, exhausted, ready to give in,
But you stand strong despite the adversity.

Decreeing, "Satan will not have my mind.
He will not have me."
GOD is the Ruler,
The Creator of everything.
He knows all about me.
I'm His creation,
Shaped and fashioned in the image
Of the King.

In the battle of the mind,
God is the Referee,
And in the end,
My hand shall be raised victoriously
Because I am a child of the KING!

The Pit of Defeat

I ask the question,
"Who has ever been in a pit,
A place so dark and deep,
Where no beam of light can be found,
And emotions are drained,
The pit where the enemy reigns?"

You look around,
And all you see is the darkness
That covers your pursuit to destiny.
Your faith feels weak.
Your strength is totally gone.
The wall of life seems to close in on you.
Chaos is all around,
And stability is nowhere to be found.

"Have you ever been in this pit?"
I ask you again.
"When you can't speak, eat or sleep,
The spirit of heaviness consumes you,
Demons torment day after day
With every emotional trick
They can send your way,

Pulling at your mind,
Trying to destroy your joy and peace inside?"
It's a cold and dreadful place,
Where hope tries to breathe,
And dreams fight to stay alive.

In this pit, nothing seems right,
But in your heart, you know you must fight.
You say to yourself,
"Just wait and see.
God will deliver me."

He is tugging at your heart,
Saying, "Recapture your mind.
Be obedient; it is better than sacrifice."

The light of the Word
Begins to come alive,
Cutting through everything
That has been a lie,
Removing darkness.

Now you are able to see the ladder,
To climb all the way up to victory.
The demons begin to tremble.
Strength has been restored.
My spirit is alive and well.

GOD continually proves He is on my side.
With His Word on the inside of me,
I began to speak victory.
GOD has turned my ashes into beauty.
I have traded the spirit of heaviness
For a garment of praise.

As I begin to rise above my circumstances,
Every word I speak brings me to the top
Of this dreadful pit
That tries to keep me in captivity.
With a sigh of relief
And a heart of thanksgiving,
I am now free,
To reign and take dominion
Over the enemy.

Thank GOD, the pit cannot hold me.
But hear the warning:
Pray and don't cease!
Satan is always looking
For an opportunity to put you back in the pit.
And it is called THE PIT OF DEFEAT!

Author Contact Page

You may contact Chelsea Johnson at the following address:

Chelsea Johnson
Antioch Christian Fellowship Worldwide
P.O. Box 77923
Baton Rouge, LA 70879

www.acfworldwide.org
Email: prophetesschelsea@gmail.com

CPSIA information can be obtained
at www.ICGtesting.com
Printed in the USA
FFOW02n1019151115
18563FF

9 781940 461410